LIVING SPACES
IN THE
DESERT

LIBRARY OF CONGRESS CATALOGING-IN-PUBLICATION DATA

Stewart, Gail, 1949-
    The deserts / by Gail B. Stewart.
        p. cm. -- (Living spaces)
    Includes index.
    ISBN 0-86592-106-7
    1. Ethnology--Juvenile literature.   2. Deserts--Juvenile literature.
3. Anthropo-geography--Juvenile literature.   4. Nomads--Juvenile
literature.   I. Title.   II. Series: Stewart, Gail, 1949-   Living spaces.
GF55.S73 1989
304.2--dc20   89-33247
                                                                    CIP
                                                                    AC

IN THE
DESERT

TEXT BY
GAIL STEWART

DESIGN & PRODUCTION BY
MARK E. AHLSTROM
(The Bookworks)

**ROURKE
ENTERPRISES,
INC.**
Vero Beach, FL 32964
U.S.A.

IN THE DESERT

TABLE OF CONTENTS

CREDITS

PHOTOS:

D.C. Clegg/FPG Int'l. ..... cover photo, 4

Megan Biesele/Anthro Photo 7

Stan Washburn/Anthro Photo 9

Irven DeVore/Anthro Photo ... 10, 12, 23

Lila AbuLughod/Anthro Photo 13

Ingo Riepl/ Anthro Photo 15

B. Worley/Anthro Photo 18, 19

Dennis Hallinan/FPG Int'l. 21

AP/Wide World Photos 26

Lee Kuhn/FPG Int'l. 29

TYPESETTING AND LAYOUT: THE FINAL WORD
PRINTING: WORZALLA PUBLISHING CO.

THE DESERT

Imagine for a moment that you are in a different place. It is afternoon, and the sun is beating down on you. The air is hot and dry.

All around you see sand and rocks. The sky is a brilliant blue. Although you'd give anything for a bit of relief from the sun, there doesn't seem to be a cloud in sight.

The wind blows, but it feels like the blast of a furnace around your face. Small particles of sand are picked up by the wind, and they lash against your skin. Your eyes water and sting.

Now imagine you are in that very same place, but it is night. The wind continues to howl, but now it feels cold—bitterly cold. There are no trees and no buildings—there is nothing to break the wind and the snarling sand. The temperature continues to drop. By dawn there will be a thin layer of frost on the rocks nearby.

This place you are imagining is called a desert. There are many deserts in the world, and although they differ in some ways, they are very much alike.

Deserts are places that are very dry. There is so little moisture, in fact, that most living things could not exist there for very long. There are plants and animals that can survive, but they have learned to adapt to very harsh conditions.

Why is there so little moisture? Most deserts are near mountains. Clouds that pass overhead usually hit the mountains and are forced upwards. Any rain that the clouds are carrying is dropped in the mountains. There is none left over to fall on the desert on the other side.

Another reason for the dryness of deserts is that most of them are near the equator. The equator is the imaginary line that rings the center of the earth. Lands near the equator are very hot—the sun's rays shine very directly on them. The sun heats up the rocks and sand until they give off heat, too.

There are sometimes rivers that run through a desert, but usually they do not. Very often underground springs lie beneath it, however. Sometimes the spring forces its way to the surface. When this happens, an area of green grass and plants grows nearby. Such an area is called an oasis, and it is a welcome sight for any desert traveler! An oasis is an opportunity to get a supply of fresh water and to cool off in the shade of a tree.

The daytime temperatures in

Deserts are hot, dry places. They can also be very beautiful!

a desert are almost always very hot. Temperatures of 120 degrees Fahrenheit are not at all unusual. The sand gets even hotter than that—sometimes 150 degrees! Yet when the sun disappears at night, the temperatures fall very fast. Sand and rocks that were burning to the touch become cold. Frost is not uncommon.

The desert, then, is a place of extremes. It is one of the most empty regions of the world—few people wish to make their homes in or near a desert. Yet for thousands of years, there have been some who have lived their lives as desert people.

Most are nomads, or wanderers. They herd sheep, or camels, or goats. They move from place to place, taking their animals from one little area of pasture to another. Some are traders, carrying foods and dry goods from one settlement to another, always looking for someone to barter with.

All of these desert nomads have adapted to very difficult, unfriendly conditions. The ways in which they have adapted are unusual and quite amazing. There are big problems to be solved. With very few natural building materials to be found, for instance, what sorts of homes do these nomads live in? How are they able to exist in the dry, parching heat and the nighttime cold of the world's deserts?

THE SAN OF THE KALAHARI

One group of people who have made their home in the desert for many thousands of years is the San, often called Bushmen. The San have learned how to exist in the dry, hot re-

San women and children go out to gather roots and grasses for food. They know which desert plants make good tea, and which ones can be made into medicines.

gions of the Kalahari Desert in southern Africa.

The San live by being hunters and gatherers. They dig in the ground for roots and grasses that are good to eat. They know what desert plants make good tea, and which ones can be made into medicines. They hunt sometimes, but hunting provides more excitement than it does food.

The Kalahari Desert is a little different from other deserts, in that it has areas of grasslands. Low, yellowish scrub grasses grow in the sand—they need almost no water to survive. The scrub grasses are a useful material for building the San homes.

A San woman of the Kalahari builds a kua, the hut in which the San families live.

The San move from place to place quite often, usually traveling in groups of 25 or 30. As soon as the water supply begins to run low, or when there are too few of the edible plants they depend on, the people move on. They do not have pack animals, such as donkeys or camels, as other desert dwellers have. Everything they own they carry themselves—that means they bring only what is absolutely vital. For the San, "vital" means an extra pair of sandals, a drum for the tribal dances, cooking utensils, and bows and arrows.

Building The Kua

When the San come to a place that has a good supply of water and edible plants, the men and older boys are in charge of clearing areas for houses. They remove grasses and other plants, so that the floor of the dwelling, called a kua, will be sandy.

Once the site is clear, however, the men are finished working. They sit together and drink tea while the women begin the long job of building the kua. Although it's possible to build a kua in an hour or two, it usually takes an entire day to construct a large, well-made dwelling.

The first step is to find tall, flexible sticks, about six feet long. The sticks are peeled and stuck into the ground, in a circle about six feet in diameter. When there are enough sticks in the sand to make the circle complete, one of the women wraps a blade of thick grass around the ends to bind them together at the top. So far, the kua looks like a round, dome-shaped cage.

The next step is to weave reeds and wide-leaved plants through the support sticks. This provides protection against the wind, and the cold night air. The final step of the building process is to make the walls and roof thicker. The women pad the kua's walls and roof with bundles of scrub grass. This provides insulation, not only from the cold, but also from the hot daytime sun.

Each family has a kua—a San settlement is made up of six or seven. Because they are low, and because they are covered with scrub grass, the kuas blend in very well with their desert surroundings. This is good, for the Bushmen are a very shy,

This kua is nearly ready for the family. The hut has been padded with scrub grass that provides insulation from the hot daytime sun and the cold at night.

private people. They are nervous when other desert people approach them. They are glad that their desert homes help them stay hidden.

A kua will last three or four months. By the time it starts to wear out, the water and food supplies will run out, too. Then it is time to move on!

THE BEDOUINS OF ARABIA

Saudi Arabia is a large country in southwestern Asia. It is separated from northeast Africa by the Red Sea. Most of Saudi

Arabia is a hot, dry wasteland called the Arabian Desert. There are no rivers, and very little vegetation. The temperature is often at 130 degrees, and the hot desert winds create dangerous sandstorms. The Arabian Desert is so harsh and unfriendly, in fact, that there are many areas of it that have never been explored.

At one time, half of the people of Saudi Arabia were Bedouins, a word which means "desert dwellers." They lived near an oasis. They herded flocks of sheep and goats, and they rode on camels. The Bedouins were traders, too. They carried with them beautiful jewelry and woven rugs that they had made. When they came to an oasis, the

Bedouin tents, like these in Egypt's Western Desert, must withstand dangerous sandstorms. The Bedouins also live in the Arabian Desert, which makes up most of the country of Saudi Arabia.

Bedouins would unfold the sacks of jewelry and crafts. People would buy things, or trade other things.

There are not as many Bedouins as there once were. Many have decided to stop wandering through the desert with their camels and their flocks. These Bedouins have begun living in villages in Saudi Arabia.

But there are still many Bedouins who are nomads. They are proud and very independent. Even when camping near a village or city, they stay on the very outskirts. They have their own way of doing things, and they dislike others telling them what to do.

The Black Tents

Bedouins in the Arabian Desert live in open-sided tents made of black goat hair. These coverings are woven by the Bedouin women on large looms that they carry with them. The tents are large—often eight or ten people live in one. That means that the covers must be very wide and very long. A cover for a tent is not one single piece; rather, it is made up of several strips that are sewn together.

The coverings are placed over long poles that have been anchored in the sand. Usually there are two or three long rows of wooden poles. Sometimes the Bedouins use wooden stakes or ropes to tie down the tent. They fasten the stakes or ropes to the strong roots of bushes underground in the desert sand.

Why do the Bedouins use black goat hair? Since black is a color that absorbs heat, wouldn't it be better to use white? The idea behind the dark tent is that black provides much thicker,

A young Bedouin girl makes tea.

denser shade. White might allow some sunlight into the tent, and make it impossible to get relief from the sun's rays.

Assembling Camp

Like the San of southern Africa, the Bedouins leave the job of setting up camp to the women. When the group of travelers, called a caravan, reaches a good place to camp, the men gather together to smoke and drink coffee. The women and children set up the tents.

Because of the fierce desert winds, it is important that the tents are tied down securely. It is also important for awnings to be placed on the tent. These can be rolled down if the night air becomes too cold, or in case of a sandstorm. The awnings are made of goat hair, too, or perhaps wool or camel hair.

Usually the tents in a caravan are laid out in two rows parallel to one another. Sometimes, however, there is the threat of bandits or raiders. In unfriendly territory, the camp is set up in a different way. The tents are arranged in an oval shape. At night, the Bedouins put their flocks and camels into the center of the oval for protection.

Inside a Bedouin Tent

The tents are each divided into two sections, one for the men and the other for the women. The "wall" that divides the tent is made of the same material as the tent covering itself.

The men's side has space for sleeping, sitting, and storing the gear needed for riding the camels. The women's side has space for sleeping, storing and cooking food, and baggage. If there were a little baby in the caravan, he or she would sleep in the women's side. A little hammock, called a hababa, would be set up for the baby.

Just outside the tent is the area for making coffee, and for weaving. The hearth fire is here, too. The fire is fueled by charcoal, scrub grasses, or even dried camel droppings.

Outside the tent the Bedouins put up T-shaped posts. These are perches for the trained falcons that many of the Bedouins have. Owning falcons is an ancient tradition among many groups of Bedouins. The birds are trained to hunt for small animals in the desert, such as rabbits or other birds. The falcon will snatch its prey with its sharp talons, or claws, and bring the catch back to its master. The animals are eaten by the Bedouins.

As with other nomadic people, the Bedouins remain in one place only for a short time. When the little patches of green grass have been eaten by their flocks, or when the water supply grows smaller, it is time to move. The women pack up the tents. The poles and heavy covers are loaded on camels for the long journey.

THE "BLUE PEOPLE" OF THE SAHARA

The Sahara is the largest desert in the world. It stretches along the northern part of Africa, from the Atlantic Ocean to the Red Sea. The Sahara covers over 3 million square miles!

The Sahara has almost none of the scrub grass and bushes that the Kalahari Desert has. Those who have seen the Sahara say that it is "sand, sand, and more sand." Indeed, it is very easy to become lost, because there are no landmarks. There are no trees and no bushes. There is nothing at all that could give a traveler a sense of direction. Sandstorms are common. Temperatures in the Sahara can range from 130 degrees at noon, to 32 degrees at night!

The Tuareg are a tribe of nomadic people who live in the Sahara. It has always been easy to recognize a Tuareg from among other desert people. All desert people wear veils over their faces to protect them from sand. The Tuareg's veils are always a bright blue. The blue

A Tuareg woman grinds millet for her family's meal.

Tuareg women construct an ehen, a tent covered by tanned goatskins. It takes about 40 goatskins to make a medium-sized ehen.

dye often rubs off on the Tuaregs' skin, giving them a blue look!

They travel throughout the Sahara. Many Tuareg raise camels. Others travel from place to place carrying a supply of salt. The salt and the camels can be traded to other people. In return, the Tuareg get tea, flour, and goatskins.

The Ehen

Why goatskins? The Tuareg are different from the Bedouins and other desert dwellers. Neither the men nor the women have learned to weave. Therefore, they do not make their homes out of woven goat hair. They use leather made from tanned goatskins to cover their homes.

The Tuareg live in tents, called ehen. The ehen is made by first putting up a frame of poles on the sand. The poles are attached to one another by rope, to form a box. The frame is then covered with skins that have been sewn together. It takes about 40 goatskins (camel skin doesn't work for tanning) to make a medium-sized ehen.

The long ends of the skins are cut into tassels. This makes the ehen look fancier. The parts of the hides from the neck or legs are attached to ropes. The Tuareg secure the ehen with ropes, just as the Bedouin do. They want to take no chances that a strong desert wind will blow their home away!

When a young man and woman get married, the bride's family always gives a gift of tent poles and the goatskin cover. It is interesting that in the Tuareg language, the word for wedding is also "ehen"!

THE ABORIGINES OF AUSTRALIA

The western third of Australia is made up of three deserts—the Great Sandy Desert, the Gibson, and the Great Victoria. Sometimes the three deserts are considered as one huge desert—the Western Desert.

The Western Desert is more colorful than the Sahara or the Kalahari. There are red and green rocks, and patches of scrub grasses that seem almost like a carpet. The ground is very flat. Everywhere there are colorful bushes. Birds of every color flit from bush to bush. The Western Desert looks like a friendly place.

But the climate of this place is severe. Temperatures climb above 130 degrees in the summer, and the nights are often cold. Desert storms and whirlwinds are common. Although the desert can go for years without getting any rain, downpours can happen. When a sudden downpour hits, the whole desert becomes flooded.

The Aborigines of Australia have been desert people for 30,000 years.

There are other dangers in the Western Desert besides the climate. Poisonous scorpions make their home here, as do many varieties of deadly snakes. Ants and flies are a problem, too. They buzz and swarm everywhere. Travelers making their way through the Western Desert have written about the "murderous" insects that never stop bothering both people and animals.

Yet there is one group of people that has lived in the Western Desert for a very long time. The Aborigines of Australia have existed as a desert people for 30,000 years!

"Invisible Houses"

Some of the Aborigines live today as their ancestors have always done. They are nomads, wandering the desert in search of water and food. By tradition, the men are the hunters, using bows and arrows and boomerangs to bring down larger game. The women and children gather berries, plants, lizards, and small birds for food.

The Aborigines build no houses at all. They have learned to survive the scorching heat by being quiet and still during the hottest part of the day. They lie in whatever shade they can find—maybe under one of the clumps of bushes found everywhere in the desert.

But because they build no houses doesn't mean they have no homes. The group that travels together sleeps in a common area. They might string branches together to form a windbreak. This provides some shade, and some shelter from the cold night winds.

The windbreak is sort of a

"home base" for the Aborigines. They have cooking fires within the windbreak. The Aborigine style of cooking is rather easy. They bake whatever game they find on a mixture of hot ashes and sand.

There are other activities that go on in the windbreak. Songs, dances, and tribal rituals have been important to the Aborigines for thousands of years. They use such rituals to remind themselves of their ancestors. They

An Aborigine camp has no houses. Aborigines who travel together sleep in a common area, where they may build a windbreak.

see the desert as a wonderful, rich place, made especially for them by gods from long ago.

Because they view the desert as a friendly place, the Aborigines have always taken good care of it. They have tried to use the desert carefully, never taking more than they need at one time. When building their windbreak, for instance, they need to break off branches from desert trees or bushes. They make certain that when they break off a branch, they don't damage the large stem of the plant.

The Modern Dwellings

As more and more white settlers have moved near the desert, some of the Aborigines have stopped being nomads. They often visit the white settlements and find that food there is plentiful. Many Aborigines have given up their lives as gatherers or hunters.

Many of the Aborigines now work on cattle ranches near the desert. The government has provided shelters for the Aborigine people. The shelters are quite simple—four poles with a roof of canvas or metal. There are no walls on these government shelters. The shelters often have rubbish or broken pieces of machinery around them, which have been dumped by the ranch owners.

The Aborigines' shelters are arranged in small groups. The groups are decided on the basis of language. There are many dialects, or varieties, of the Aborigine language. People want to live near those who speak the same dialect. The Aborigines move their shelters when the area nearby becomes too cluttered or dirty.

The Aborigines who live in these settlements buy food at the little stores nearby. Most of the families still cook their meals in the traditional way, however, on hot ashes and sand.

THE NAVAJO OF THE AMERICAN SOUTHWEST

The southwestern part of the United States contains a lot of desert. It is good land for rattlesnakes, coyotes, and cacti—these living things don't need much water to survive. But it is hard for people to live here.

The Navajo are a large group of Native Americans. They have lived in the deserts of Arizona for thousands of years. They are the largest of all the American Indian nations. Today, there are more than 125,000 Navajo.

Like almost every other desert people, the Navajo are nomads. Many of them herd sheep, and must move from pasture to pasture. More than any other Native Americans, the Navajo people have held to their traditional ways. They eat, dress, and worship their gods in many of the same ways their ancestors did. They also continue to build their houses in traditional ways.

The Hogan

Although the building materials have changed over the years, the style of the Navajo home has stayed the same. The house is called a hogan. It has eight sides, and is dome-shaped.

Early Navajo built their hogans out of bent poles. The ends of the poles were stuck in

25

the ground and tied together where they crossed at the top. Smaller poles were added between the large poles. Then the whole frame was packed down with mud and sand. This provided warmth from the cold night air and a shady shelter from the hot sun. A hole was left in the roof. This was to allow smoke from the family's hearth fire to escape.

Hogans today are still eight-sided, but they are built of sod, sandstone, or even cinder blocks. They have no windows, but there is still an opening in the roof.

Navajo families must move from time to time because of their sheep, so they often have several different hogans. Family members carry their belongings with them. They know that

Navajo women weave a rug near their traditional home, the hogan. Some Navajos live in stone houses with windows.

when they get to the next grazing pasture, they will have a good strong home waiting for them. They do not worry about other people using their empty hogans—to use another's home would be bad luck.

Religion and the Hogan

For the Navajo, the hogan is not merely a shelter. It is also the center of religion. There are very specific steps the Navajo family must follow when building the hogan. To not follow these steps would be an insult to the gods.

For one thing, the entrance to the hogan must always face east. The entrance may be a wooden door or a heavy woolen blanket, decorated with sacred symbols. When they walk into the hogan, men are expected to sit on the north side. The women, on the other hand, sit on the south side. All of the women's belongings are on the south side of the hogan—the cooking pots, the weaving looms, and so on. The west side of the hogan is reserved for guests.

Navajo children play as loudly and roughly as any other children, and that's fine. But when they enter the hogan, they know that the rough play stops. The hogan is not a place for horseplay or loud talk. It is a quiet, special place where a family can be together.

There are even special ways of entering a hogan, according to the Navajo religion. When someone comes into the hogan, he or she must follow what is called the "sunwise path." This means that the movement must follow the path of the sun, from east to west, in a clockwise direction. It is bad manners to step across the hearth, or to step over someone sleeping or sitting on the floor.

The floor of the hogan becomes very important when a family member is sick. Special holy men, called hosteen, are called in. They bring with them many sacks, each containing sand of a different color. The hosteen use the sand to create a colorful picture on the floor. The picture may be a design, or pictures of things important to the sick person. When the picture is done, the sick person is carried and placed in the center of the design. The Navajo believe that this can help make the person well again.

The Navajo religion has a name for the god of death. He is called Chindi, and he is very, very powerful. When a Navajo dies, it is believed that Chindi has entered the hogan, and has taken the person away. A hogan which Chindi has entered is considered bad luck. No one will live in a hogan where someone has died.

If the grandfather of the family dies, for example, the other family members pack up their things and move out. The family builds another hogan, perhaps nearby. The grandfather's body is taken out of the hogan for burial, but not through the door. A wall is broken along the north side, and the body is removed that way. The empty hogan will just stand there, year after year. Eventually, it will begin to fall apart and collapse.

A FINAL THOUGHT

There are many people who live in the desert. In some ways, the people are very different from each other. Some of the people have very few possessions. They have no pack animals, so they keep only what is easy to carry from place to place. Many of these people build no houses at all; others make houses that are only used for a few months.

There are other people who carry their homes with them. They have pack animals, such as camels, to transport tent coverings and poles from place to place. There are still other people whose homes are not meant to be moved. These homes are used from time to time for many years.

The homes of the desert dwellers are alike in one important way. They are all made out of materials that can be easily found or traded for. Traditions have helped all of these people create the best ways of surviving in a harsh climate.

These cliff dwellings at Mesa Verde National Park in southwestern Colorado were once the homes of a prehistoric people. For centuries, desert people have been adapting to their environment.

GLOSSARY

Aborigine—one of a very old group of people who have made their home in the Western Desert of Australia.

ancestors—grandparents, great grandparents, and others in your family who come before you.

Bedouin—a desert dweller in Saudi Arabia.

Bushmen—another name for the San of the Kalahari Desert.

caravan—a group of desert people traveling together, usually on camels.

Chindi—the Navajo god of death.

desert—one of the earth's regions. Deserts are usually very hot and dry.

dialect—one variety of a certain language.

ehen—the tent of the Tuareg people.

equator—imaginary line circling the earth.

hababa—a small hammock for a baby in a Bedouin tent.

hogan—traditional Navajo house.

hosteen—a holy man of the Navajo people.

kua—Bushman home made of poles and reeds.

Navajo—Native American desert people of Arizona.

nomad—a wanderer.

oasis—a small area of green plants and trees found in the desert.

Sahara—the largest desert in the world. The Sahara is in northern Africa.

San—desert people of the Kalahari Desert in southern Africa.

talon—the claw of a falcon.

tanned—animal skin that is heated and dried to make leather.

tradition—a custom handed down through generations.

Tuareg—one tribe of desert people of the Sahara.

INDEX